BATHILDA

Borgo Press Books by ALEXANDRE DUMAS

Anthony
The Barricade at Clichy; or, The Fall of Napoleon
Bathilda
Caligula
The Corsican Brothers (with Eugène Grangé & Xavier de Montépin)
The Count of Monte Cristo, Part One: The Betrayal of Edmond Dantès
The Count of Monte Cristo, Part Two: The Resurrection of Edmond Dantès
The Count of Monte Cristo, Part Three: The Rise of Monte Cristo
The Count of Monte Cristo, Part Four: The Revenge of Monte Cristo
A Fairy Tale (with Adolphe de Leuven & Léon Lhérie)
The Gold Thieves (with Countess Céleste de Chabrillan)
Kean
The Last of the Three Musketeers; or, The Prisoner of the Bastille (Musketeers #3)
Lorenzino
The Mad Marquis (with Emmanuel Théaulon & Ernest Jaime)
The Mohicans of Paris
Napoléon Bonaparte
Queen Margot
Richard Darlington (with Prosper Dinaux)
Sylvandire
The Three Musketeers (Musketeers #1)
The Three Musketeers—Twenty Years Later (Musketeers #2)
The Tower of Death (with Frédéric Gaillardet)
The Two Dianas (with Paul Meurice)
Urbain Grandier and the Devils of Loudon
The Venetian
The Whites and the Blues
The Widow's Husband; and, Porthos in Search of an Outfit
Young Louix XIV

RELATED DRAMAS:

The Queen's Necklace, by Pierre Decourcelle
The Seed of the Musketeers, by Paul de Kock & Guénée (Musketeers #5)
The San Felice, by Maurice Drack
The Son of Porthos the Musketeer, by Émile Blavet (Musketeers #4)
A Summer Night's Dream, Adolphe de Leuven & Joseph-Bernard Rosier
The Widow's Husband; and, Porthos in Search of an Outfit: Two Dumasian Comedies, edited by Frank J. Morlock

BATHILDA

A PLAY IN THREE ACTS

ALEXANDRE DUMAS

Translated and Adapted by Frank J. Morlock

THE BORGO PRESS
MMXIII

BATHILDA

Copyright © 2004, 2013 by Frank J. Morlock

FIRST BORGO PRESS EDITION

Published by Wildside Press LLC

www.wildsidebooks.com

DEDICATION

To my doctor, Timothy Krohe,

with appreciation for the care he's given me.

CONTENTS

CAST OF CHARACTERS	9
ACT I	11
ACT II	77
ACT III	131
ABOUT THE AUTHOR	157

CAST OF CHARACTERS

Bathilda d'Illières

Marcel

Lucien Deworde

Guilaumin

François, a valet

Germaine, Bathilda's maid

A Domino (female)

ACT I

The stage represents a small room. To the left, the room of Madame d'Illières—facing it, on the right, a window—further back, to the left, a service stairway, facing it, Germaine's room. Door in the middle.

AT RISE, Germaine is knitting a tapestry by a round table at the left.

FRANÇOIS

Say there, Mme Germaine!

GERMAINE

Well—

FRANÇOIS

See there—in the street—a young man who keeps looking over here.

GERMAINE

That's someone who's spying, as there are many folk

of my acquaintance.

FRANÇOIS

(aside)

That's for me—that is, thank you very much—

(aloud)

It's that he can't take his eye off the window—

GERMAINE

What is it you are doing?

FRANÇOIS

Why he's very well covered—come have a look.

GERMAINE

Mind your business and not what's going on in the street—curious.

(she goes to look)

Mr. Marcel again!

FRANÇOIS

Mr. Marcel—Ah! You know him—you see plainly that I didn't do so bad by disturbing you.

GERMAINE

What do you mean by that? I don't know him.

FRANÇOIS

He's familiar, in that case; see his making signs to you—good! Good! He's crossing the street, he's rapping at the hotel—do you hear?

GERMAINE

My God!

FRANÇOIS

Ah! Oh! Dame Germaine, you didn't mention you have intrigues with young folks in cloaks.

GERMAINE

Imbecile!

FRANÇOIS

It's not you then, it's Madame, it's certainly not for me that this gentleman is coming here.

GERMAINE

And who told you he's coming here?

FRANÇOIS

Heavens: I hear him in the antechamber.

GERMAINE

Get out of here, you've finished your work.

FRANÇOIS

A private meeting—nothing more than that; I'm clearing out, Madame Germaine.

GERMAINE

(indicating a service stairway)

This way, if you please.

FRANÇOIS

Oh, you're afraid I'll meet him—better and better.

GERMAINE

Go and don't argue, or I'll complain to Madame.

FRANÇOIS

Ah! That's the way it is—I'll complain to Madame! Because you are her nurse, you think everything is permitted—you are going to Madame. Well, as for me,

I'm going to warn Mr. Deworde, ah!

(He leaves.)

GERMAINE

Will you get going! He is such a tattletale.

(Enter Marcel.)

GERMAINE

My God! Mr. Marcel, is it you?

MARCEL

What's astonishing about that? Have you forgotten me, too?

GERMAINE

No, but I would not be able to recognize you, you've changed so much! Poor child! Look, what have you come to find here—? Madame, right? Still? Well! She no longer wants to see you, she no longer thinks of you—it's useless.

MARCEL

She's more happy?

GERMAINE

At least that's what she says—

MARCEL

I have to speak to her.

GERMAINE

That's quite difficult, my dear child.

MARCEL

I must speak to her, I tell you—

GERMAINE

She was hoping you'd returned to Tours—

MARCEL

Yes. But I've come back. My mother is dead, Germaine.

GERMAINE

My God!

MARCEL

Yes, Guilaumin, that brave lad you knew!

GERMAINE

Who kept me company during your long strolls in the park with Madame—brave lad—but he didn't have a very strong head.

MARCEL

Well, I left him with my mother. He wrote me twenty times that she was unwell, then ill, then despairing, without being able to tear me away from here, so long as I was kept here by my mad passion—finally one of his last letters carried me away. I was ashamed of myself, of leaving my mother this way, abandoned to the care of a stranger—I left my poor mother. I got there to receive her last sigh.

It was when I had lost her, Germaine, that I noticed that I ought to have been able to see all the days this good mother had loved me, she, with that profound and infinite love which resisted everything—so different from the other sort of love—and instead of staying near her, I abandoned her—for whom? For a flirt, you see, Germaine, for a woman who didn't love me, who in her widowhood, her solitude, her exile, found me there, noticed I was a bit less ridiculous than my compatriots, and did not suspect that her caprice of a day would cause the misfortune of my entire life.

Ah, my mother! When I think that I almost left her to die alone, to follow distantly in the steps of the woman who rewards me like this. Hold on, Germaine, I have here something that resembles remorse, but I won't place this remorse in my heart for nothing.

I've come back to Paris to see Bathilda—I will see her—this time there's no longer any human consideration that can hold me back. The rights that a woman gives over herself—

GERMAINE

Stop, Mr. Marcel—these rights have never been of a nature to authorize so relentless a pursuit.

MARCEL

She said that, right?

GERMAINE

And for you to deny it would not be the act of an honest man, Mr. Marcel—because I know too well the child that I raised to believe anything you could say.

MARCEL

So, Germaine, I will tell you only one thing—I must see Bathilda again—

GERMAINE

Ah! My God! You make me tremble for her.

MARCEL

And you are wrong. She has nothing to fear if she receives me. No, you see, jealousy no longer carries me away to—I don't know what. And her love of before—for you know she did love me—

GERMAINE

Alas! Yes! I know it—but that love of which you speak has disappeared, suddenly, as if she was ashamed of it, and every time I wanted to speak to her of you, she imposed silence on me. So what happened? You tell me, since she doesn't want to tell me.

MARCEL

Nothing.

GERMAINE

Oh! I am quite sure of the contrary. You must have caused her some great pain.

MARCEL

What do I care about the past? Germaine, from all I can tell, it's she who no longer loves me; and as for me, I still love her—well, give her some advice—it's not to treat me the way she's doing, as she would treat a nobody. I am made up of extremes—there's as much good as bad in me—and trust me: all the world could not say as much. So then, I am going to see her right now.

GERMAINE

I didn't say a word about that.

MARCEL

Yes, but I said it, my good Germaine!

(Ringing.)

MARCEL

What, there's Bathilda ringing—proving she is visible— Well! Announce me.

GERMAINE

Listen; it's impossible for you to enter—so, trust me, your good Germaine, who still loves you like a second child, which is perhaps bad, but something she cannot help, be reasonable; go away—I will go bring you news.

MARCEL

Not at all, since I've come this far, I will wait for it.

GERMAINE

Why, are you mad?

MARCEL

On the contrary, I am beginning to be sane.

GERMAINE

God! I hear Madame.

MARCEL

Ah! At last.

GERMAINE

Look—for me, Mr. Marcel, I entreat you, for me, a poor woman who would be ruined if I were obliged to separate from Bathilda, for me who's never done anything to you—and who cannot thus present you to her without giving her time to forewarn her, to excuse myself. If you want me to give you the word, go into my room—I will rap when the time comes.

MARCEL

I will gladly do it, but think that I won't leave without having seen her, without having spoken to her? Where's your room?

GERMAINE

(opening the side door)

There, there at the end of the corridor—go—thanks my child—go—go—and not a word, right? Wait for me, you promise me?

MARCEL

As for me, I am promising nothing—everything depends on the circumstances.

GERMAINE

Will you go, bad boy—bullhead!

(Marcel goes.)

GERMAINE

Just in time!

BATHILDA

What's going on in this house that no one comes when I call, neither you nor Josephine?

GERMAINE

Josephine went to the fashion shop—and as for me, I was busy.

BATHILDA

Meaning you didn't want to come when I rang, right? To make me remember you are not a chamber maid and that I must call you differently from the servants. Don't worry, my good Germaine. I am not forgetting it. Nor am I coming to demand a new proof of your eternal devotion.

GERMAINE

Oh! Whatever you wish, you know that well, Madame.

BATHILDA

(sitting)

It's that I need your devotion and even your advice.

GERMAINE

My advice? You want to laugh!

BATHILDA

No, no, I am in a cruel situation! I need someone to watch over me, to take an authority over my heart that my dying mother didn't transmit to anyone—that my husband exercised as a friend—like a father. Also, you know, if despite the difference in our ages, I had a single sin, a mere thought to reproach myself with during all the time he lived; and then he died and I find myself alone again.

GERMAINE

And Mr. Deworde, his nephew, who loved you so much, and to whom he commended you, or rather bequeathed you—are you forgetting him?

BATHILDA

No, I'm not forgetting him, and I have for Deworde more than just gratitude, but Deworde was in England when my husband died, too occupied with his industrial establishments to return to France to watch over a poor widow. So I remained for six months, Germaine; then one of those fatal things happened to me which place in question the happiness of an entire life.

GERMAINE

Great God! What Mr. Marcel allowed me to suspect—could it be true?

BATHILDA

Marcel let you suspect something, ah!

GERMAINE

My dear child! In the name of heaven, have confidence in me.

BATHILDA

I have nothing to reproach myself with, Germaine. Let that suffice for you.

GERMAINE

And that's all I want to know. My God! But why are you afraid of him, then, if you have nothing to reproach yourself with?

BATHILDA

Now, that's where lies the secret I cannot tell you, Germaine—but I have reasons to fear him— For a long while I deceived myself on his account; what I had taken in him for love was passion; what I thought was jealousy was egoism. Marcel is capable of anything, not through love, but through pride; he would see me at his feet but would have no pity on me. Can you imagine that if I had not acquired the conviction of what I just told you, I would have refused to marry him? He's not rich, but I am—and enough for two.

GERMAINE

Still, he loved you with all his heart. Remember the day he exposed his life to save yours.

BATHILDA

Never speak to me of that day—from that day my

misfortune dates—it would have been better for him to let me die than to save me at that price! Germaine—never a word which reminds me of that day—never.

GERMAINE

I will obey you, although I don't understand your problem at all; but then, if you separated him from all hope, why is he following you around everywhere?

BATHILDA

That's precisely what frightens me. If Deworde noticed that a man was ceaselessly on my trail, following me to church, on strolls, what would he think of such assiduity? I was hoping to have some release; for the last month I haven't noticed him. Yesterday I found him again at the Opera—at the back of a pit-box. Heavens, what can I tell you, Germaine? I have a foreboding that all this will end badly.

GERMAINE

My God! My God! What to do?

BATHILDA

Well, Germaine, you must go find him. Do you know where he lives?

GERMAINE

Certainly, but what will I tell him?

BATHILDA

Make him understand that in returning to society, I need all that consideration without which a woman cannot live, and that he will ruin me by such obstinacy—let him forget me. My God, he will find thousands of women prettier than I am. What have I got which attaches here to my person like this?

GERMAINE

I am really afraid of accomplishing nothing.

BATHILDA

You will pray; you will entreat; at bottom he's not bad.

GERMAINE

Shouldn't you see him yourself?

BATHILDA

Oh! Never! If Deworde knew of it, at the point we've reached where this very evening I promised to announce to his friends our imminent marriage— No, Germaine, no—when I met Marcel for the first time, there was no question as yet of anything between me and Deworde.

I could therefore love him without crime, and I do not owe Deworde an account of my conduct until the day when I accepted his pretensions. But from that day, I intend to remain pure, even in thought, and therefore I mustn't see Marcel again. Besides, I love Deworde, you see, and to see Marcel again would be impossible for me.

GERMAINE

Ah! My God!

BATHILDA

Well! What, don't you dare go to his place?

GERMAINE

That's not it.

BATHILDA

What is it, then?

GERMAINE

It's that he won't want to leave Paris.

BATHILDA

Still, he must leave, or if he doesn't, then I will.

GERMAINE

You—

BATHILDA

No question. If the least rumor of this marriage reached him before all was consummated, I would be lost, he would do anything to prevent it, and then, you see, there would no longer be any happiness for me.

GERMAINE

But wouldn't it be more terrible for you still if he learned of it afterwards?

BATHILDA

If he no longer has any hope, perhaps he'll be discouraged. What he would do then would be a vengeance without excuse. I think he's too decent a man to ruin me with no other end but to destroy me, and when he knows that I can no longer return to him— Go, my good Germaine, go—

GERMAINE

Madame!

BATHILDA

Well?

GERMAINE

Oh! You are going to scold me, but I swear to you it's not my fault.

BATHILDA

What?

GERMAINE

He begged me so much!

BATHILDA

Then you've seen him?

GERMAINE

Yes.

BATHILDA

Where?

GERMAINE

Here.

BATHILDA

Here, wretched woman! Here! Marcel here! Who let him in?

GERMAINE

He came—

BATHILDA

Oh! My God! But he listened to reason, didn't he? He left, promising not to return?

GERMAINE

He's here.

BATHILDA

Here, where?

GERMAINE

In my room.

BATHILDA

In your room?

GERMAINE

Happily, Mr. Deworde is in Sevigny for the whole day.

BATHILDA

Yes, for if he was here, I would be lost! Oh, my God! What to do? Yes, you are right, it is indeed lucky that

Deworde is absent, that will give us time.

FRANÇOIS

(enters, announcing)

Mr. Deworde.

BATHILDA

Great God!

GERMAINE

Mercy!

BATHILDA

(to Deworde)

What? What? It's you yourself, in truth.

DEWORDE

Well! Yes, it's me, dear Bathilda. What's so astonishing about that?

BATHILDA

Nothing—on the contrary, but you said you were forced to go to the country today, and I surely didn't count on the pleasure of seeing you until tonight.

DEWORDE

I thought it was very selfish of me to leave you with all the boredom of this ball, and to come only to profit from its pleasures, so that I am rushing to put myself at your disposition for the whole day.

BATHILDA

Ah! That's charming and very nice of you! But everything is finished.

DEWORDE

There are still letters on the table. Haven't you prepared all your invitations?

BATHILDA

Indeed, sir, and unless you don't have any to add to them—

DEWORDE

Just one, for a relative who is coming to me from Tours, a provincial that's being sent to me for me tp polish into shape.

BATHILDA

Bring him, that's the simplest thing.

DEWORDE

Well! That's what I'm going to do, with your permission.

BATHILDA

Aren't you almost master here? Do as if you already were.

DEWORDE

You are charming.

(aside)

What did that imbecile François tell me?

BATHILDA

Well, since you are here, my friend—go into the salons so as to see how the drapes are being hung. You know how much these men need to be directed by a man of taste; as for me, I have to finish dressing—then a letter to write to my sister who is ill—

DEWORDE

Truly! Claire—

BATHILDA

Yes, I received letters from Flurry.

DEWORDE

Is it dangerous?

BATHILDA

I hope not—go, so I can get ready on time.

DEWORDE

You are giving me carte-blanche?

BATHILDA

Would you like written authority?

DEWORDE

Not at all—I believe all you are telling me—because you say so—

BATHILDA

Then get going—

DEWORDE

Goodbye! Can I dispose of François?

BATHILDA

Certainly.

(She rings, François enters.)

DEWORDE

Well, go to my place, and if a young man from Tours comes to ask for me, bring him here. I will present him to you immediately—here—and this will be one less thing to do this evening. You'll excuse me?

BATHILDA

What do you think?

DEWORDE

(aside)

This François is stupid with his visions.

GERMAINE

(opening the small door)

Has he gone?

BATHILDA

He's gone, but only for a few minutes.

GERMAINE

Has he left the hotel?

BATHILDA

No—he's here in the salons.

GERMAINE

Oh! My God! And here's Mr. Marcel who's getting impatient, no question, and who is opening the door.

BATHILDA

Make a sign to him.

GERMAINE

Ah well, yes!

BATHILDA

Then, at least go this way so that Deworde doesn't reenter without our being forewarned.

GERMAINE

So I'm on my way.

(She leaves.)

BATHILDA

Oh! I am half dead.

MARCEL

I understand the effect my presence produced on you, as you have avoided the thing as long as possible.

BATHILDA

Because the determination with which you sought this interview indicates to me the decision taken to be without pity for me.

MARCEL

Madame, you ought to have recognized at the same time the impossibility of my living without seeing you. You would then be close to the truth, while doing me less injury.

BATHILDA

Sir, your first care—and perhaps I ought to say you first duty—was to take pity on the woman who owes all past sorrows to you, and who will probably owe you all her pains to come. You haven't thought you must do it, that's fine—you've forced me to see you—you have something to say to me—speak—I'm listening.

MARCEL

Bathilda—do I have the air of an enemy for you to receive me like this?

BATHILDA

Actually, I am calm. Why do you wish me ill?—I've never done anything to you.

MARCEL

Don't say that, Bathilda—because I could make you really miserable before making you suffer a thousandth part of what I have suffered. It's reached the point, Bathilda, that my love for you, and God knows I love you, is ready to turn to hate.

BATHILDA

Hate? The word is strange on your part. It seems to me that if one of the two of us has the right to hate, it's me, and yet, I don't hate you, sir.

MARCEL

Pardon! But I am embittered by suffering, unfortunate, very unfortunate. Believe me, all this through you. After you no longer loved me, something broke in me which disrupted my whole life.

What? I'm unaware of it; only I know that if you once

again said to me, "Marcel, I love you," I would become gentle and calm as a child, a word that's nothing, a word is so easy to say! You used to say that word to me—! You used to say that word to me! Well, say it again, and I will have no law except yours, no will except yours, no life except yours. My God, you are deceived on my account; what you took to be a threat was only a prayer.

You complain that I've followed you, persecuted you, watched you. A miser does as much for his treasure. You are my only riches, my only happiness. Also, when I think that I can ruin you, that I have ruined you, for I have no more than very little hope; Bathilda, wait, I'm becoming mad! But not the way you that you think—I'm unaware what these women are hiding from me—all, the same, know one thing: you can keep me at a distance, but you cannot make me give up my place. If you are not mine, Bathilda—hear what I am telling you—you will never belong to anyone else. I have rights and I will maintain them.

BATHILDA

Rights, sir! You speak of your rights! Must I remind you of how you acquired those rights? I loved my husband when I was barely twenty. He'd been a father rather than a spouse to me. At my mother's I'd never had the occasion to go into society. Hardly had a word of love came to my ear. I saw you in my château of La Touraine where I'd gone to seek the solitude of a widow.

There, for the first time, I heard an unknown, new, intoxicating language spoken. I believed you, I loved you, I thought for a moment I could deliver to you the happiness of my whole life. I confided in you as a brother, as a friend, as in the end an honest man; this confidence ruined me.

Unsuspectingly, in our long trips on the water, I spent whole hours listening to you, and in default of my mouth, my heart responded to you. One evening, lost in this reverie I was sharing, you forgot the care of the boat; it was night, it bumped into a rock and capsized. I uttered a scream, it was a goodbye to the world for I thought myself lost. I fainted, thinking to die happy, dying pure. I came to myself, you had saved my life and stolen my honor, you did not trust in my love, you sought to bind me to you through shame. I forgave you, that's all that I could do. But I no longer loved you.

Now, dare speak of your rights, sir, there they are! Are they those that an honest men can boast of, I ask you? Now what do you want with me? Why are you pursuing me like this for the six months since I left Tours? What have you come to do at my place? You are coming to compromise me, you are ruining me.

MARCEL

Me, mine, you, me, compromising you by speaking to

you? I don't understand you.

BATHILDA

Why, just think of it, I am surrounded by my family; I even have in Paris an aunt who is Superior of the Convent of the Visitation, a woman of strict morals, who, on a mere suspicion would cease to receive me. I have my servants, my employees, all around me, these natural enemies one is forced to constantly treat with caution, who only need a word to guess the truth about all this. Why, your presence here can be funereal for me, sir, to murder my reputation, that's all—and you are astonished that I'm afraid? Look, do I have to beg you?

MARCEL

You are right, but I am not insisting on being received by you. In Tours I didn't go to the château. We met each other; but then you loved me, and when one loves one fears neither family, nor relatives, nor servants; one fears only one thing, that's to no longer be loved. Well! Bathilda, cannot we meet in Paris as we did in Tours? No one is spying on your actions. If you don't dare say anything to Germaine, I have a friend in whom I can confide.

BATHILDA

Marcel, you won't be satisfied until I am ruined. A

friend, a confidant? Why see where you're dragging me!

MARCEL

A confidant who has never seen, who never will see your face, who has never known, who never will know your name, is not an indiscreet person much to be feared— Promise me that you will see me again, Bathilda, that you won't force me to employ the means I used today, which are now more repulsive to me than they are frightening to you, promise me.

GERMAINE

(entering, in Bathilda's ear)

Mr. Deworde!

BATHILDA

Great God!

Marcel

What's wrong with you?

BATHILDA

A visit, a relative of Mr. d'Illières, one of the men, you understand, consequently from whom I most vividly wish to distance suspicions.

MARCEL

Well, a promise and I am withdrawing.

BATHILDA

How pitilessly you abuse my position.

MARCEL

(violently)

Oh! Now, that's what makes me tremble, it's that I'm forced to exact—

BATHILDA

Silence! Silence! Don't speak so loud, one doesn't speak this way to a woman unless one has the right to do so—and that right, to the eyes of those less clairvoyant, how is it acquired?

MARCEL

One word and I'll withdraw; if not—

BATHILDA

(haughtily)

Well!

MARCEL

Well, I'm staying. You will present me to your relative.

BATHILDA

I will go, sir.

MARCEL

You are saying that to me in a strange manner.

BATHILDA

I am saying it to you as a woman that is forced. Don't insist any further, see, they're coming.

MARCEL

And when will I have the honor of seeing you?

BATHILDA

Tomorrow.

MARCEL

How will I know the time?

BATHILDA

Germaine will tell you.

(Deworde appears.)

BATHILDA

Goodbye, Mr. Marcel.

MARCEL

(bowing)

Madame, I have the honor.

(The two men meet at the door and bow. Marcel leaves.)

DEWORDE

(watching him move away)

Could this be the man François told me of? Marcel, I don't know that name.

BATHILDA

(moved)

Ah! Here you are! Well, what's wrong with you?

DEWORDE

Nothing, I was looking at that gentleman who's leaving?

BATHILDA

How do you like the hangings?

DEWORDE

Very elegant, you gave him his leave abruptly, it seems to me.

BATHILDA

He's an unfortunate and I wanted to be alone with you. And the flowers?

DEWORDE

Very fresh. Why is he an unfortunate and then, if he's an unfortunate, why do you receive him?

BATHILDA

My God! I receive him as I receive everybody; life is composed of small duties that are almost all boring.

DEWORDE

Still, you had some business with that young man?

BATHILDA

None. Do you have a pretty costume for my ball?

DEWORDE

I will be in a simple frock coat, dear friend. You would laugh very much to see me decked out in some costume, even more grotesque than it would be pretentious. No, I take it as a principle to avoid all opportunities to be ridiculous in the eyes of persons that I love. Ridicule suffices to damage friendships and kill love! Then, oughtn't you announce our marriage to our friends? The way of presenting them a future spouse as an astrologer or harlequin?

BATHILDA

Oh! That step is really remarkable and very decisive. Suppose we were to wait?

DEWORDE

Wasn't it agreed?

BATHILDA

No doubt; but on reflection—

DEWORDE

You repent of being engaged to me, and you don't want to engage yourself in front of others?

BATHILDA

Who told you that, dear Lucien? But what's the good of so many indifferent folks being in the secret of our happiness? It seems to me that placing it like this at the mercy of the crowd profanes it.

DEWORDE

You fear publication, Madame. There's no question something in this timidity that charms me; were it not that since this morning, I confess, I saw in you a change which worries me, your manners are no longer the same, your eyes seem always to be looking for or fleeing from something.

Listen, dear Bathilda, surely you don't suspect my affection for you, wife of my uncle, to whom I owe everything because my mother and my father died without fortune. I saw you at this home; I cannot tell you what your appearance, first of all, then your grace, then your kindness, produced on my heart, I didn't dare stop to examine the feeling I was experiencing. Madame d'Illières ought to be sacred to me. I could adore her as a divinity, not love her as a woman, I left for England when the benefactions of my uncle permitted me to found a large establishment. This establishment was at the height of its prosperity when I learned that my uncle had just died, commending to me his young wife who he left isolated and alone, I sold everything, Bathilda, I came back intending to be a brother and a friend for you, I didn't dare speak of a bolder intention. Perhaps you've encouraged me. I offered a support more real, more direct—you accepted it. A word from you, Bathilda, made me that happiest of men, but only because I thought to see that word was said to me in all the freedom of your heart. From the moment it's not that way, nothing is agreed, nothing is done; a regret on your mind today will tomorrow be a remorse in your heart. That cannot, that must not be. Be frank, Bathilda, even were your frankness to render me unhappy, I prefer to suffer than to fear, to be certain of my sorrow than to doubt your love.

BATHILDA

Why have I told you anything that resembles this? And can't you understand, Deworde, that at the approach of such a moment one experience a strange and unfamiliar emotion? Yes, unfamiliar, sir, for you cannot imagine that I experienced it. When, at the age of sixteen, they came to take me from the convent where my aunt had raised me to announce to me I was going to marry Mr. d'Illières—

Then, you see, Lucien, since that time I lived in the world! I've seen it full of envious and miscreant beings who lie in wait for your happiness to tear it to shreds, as soon as you let it escape. What do you want? Perhaps it's a folly. I feel ill at ease, I want to be far from here, It seem to me that I would love you more if we'd changed country and skies!

DEWORDE

Marvelous! I ask nothing better than to travel, since I'd be taking you with me. But a trip is only possible once everything is settled; you can only follow a husband.

BATHILDA

Yes, well! I'd like to be able to follow you instantly. You love me, Lucien, but perhaps it may be necessary to kill that love? A suspicion, a slander.

DEWORDE

And who would dare to slander you, you so good and so pure?

BATHILDA

An enemy.

DEWORDE

Why, who could be your enemy?

BATHILDA

Eh! My God! Who knows? A man has an enemy, he seeks him, he discovers him, he waits for him or goes to find him, he attacks him or defends himself; but a woman, what can she do? One blows a lie in her face, and she is tarnished and often ruined.

DEWORDE

You are sinister today. This visit of this morning has bothered you a lot, I can see that. Caused by this Mr. Marcel?

BATHILDA

Marcel? Where did you learn his name?

DEWORDE

It was you yourself who named him, when taking leave of him.

BATHILDA

No, it's not exactly that young man who tormented me, I swear to you, no, it's the world in general. And then my sister fell ill at the very moment when I was going to give the ball.

DEWORDE

Could you have received more recent news?

BATHILDA

Yes.

DEWORDE

And she's in greater danger?

BATHILDA

She's more ill, at least.

DEWORDE

You are hiding something from me.

BATHILDA

No, I'm not hiding anything from you.

DEWORDE

Is it then, only this illness, which from the gay person you were yesterday, is making you sad today?

BATHILDA

Yes, it worries me horribly, this contrast of my sister being ill in the depths of Normandy while I am giving a ball in Paris.

DEWORDE

Well, would you like me to tell you what to do, my dear Bathilda?

BATHILDA

Oh, tell me, Lucien, and I will do it.

DEWORDE

After the ball, leave for Flurry.

BATHILDA

Yes, yes, you are right, quick, leave Paris, I will leave at midnight.

DEWORDE

That appears to me to be the right of a mistress of a house. Do you know something, Bathilda? It's that you have the air of wanting to escape me.

BATHILDA

If you are jealous, what can I tell you?

DEWORDE

Me, jealous?

BATHILDA

Then I will stay.

DEWORDE

Why, no; besides, in two or three days, can't I go meet you?

BATHILDA

Oh! That's true, and our marriage? Well! Our marriage—is there an imperious need to celebrate it in Paris? Can't it done down there, in silence and mystery? Will we be less happy because no one will know of our happiness?

DEWORDE

Ah! There you are back, charming and good as always. Am I asking Paris of you? What matters in what part of the world you say yes to me? Where you swear to love me forever? It's agreed, you will leave with Germaine after the ball, and in three days, I will join you.

BATHILDA

Will you take care of ordering the horses?

DEWORDE

Certainly!

BATHILDA

Of watching to see that the carriage will be in the court

in two hours?

DEWORDE

No question.

BATHILDA

Well! Go, go busy yourself with all these details.

DEWORDE

But, Good God! We have time.

BATHILDA

Oh, if you knew how relieved and happy I am.

DEWORDE

You don't need to tell me, I see it plainly.

BATHILDA

I am so happy to leave this Paris that I detest.

DEWORDE

Yesterday you were unable to do without it.

BATHILDA

Is that a reproach?

DEWORDE

Eh! No, aren't you adorable even in your caprices?

BATHILDA

Go, if you are beginning to spoil me like that!

DEWORDE

I am not spoiling you, I am happy with your present happiness, and my future happiness, that's all.

BATHILDA

Then do all that you can to accelerate it. Go for the passports, go for the horses, go and return quickly to help me.

DEWORDE

Your hand! I'm on my way, Bathilda.

FRANÇOIS

(entering)

The relative of the gentleman is here.

DEWORDE

What relative?

FRANÇOIS

(to Deworde)

Why, the gentleman from Tours you told me to bring—

BATHILDA

(uneasy)

Someone from Tours?

DEWORDE

Ah! It's true! Bathilda, will you excuse me, it's this relative who's coming to me from the provinces and who wants to see Parisian society. He begged me to introduce him to my friends, and I am going to present him to you.

BATHILDA

But I am in a bit too intimate a negligee, and all the more good for you—! A stranger? It's impossible that I receive him thus; two minutes and I am with you.

DEWORDE

I'll give you five, go.

(Bathilda leaves.)

DEWORDE

François, show him in.

FRANÇOIS

(announcing)

Mr. Guilaumin.

GUILAUMIN

(entering)

Ah! There are you are at last. My, my, my, do you have two domiciles? Because of the National Guard, right?

DEWORDE

No, my dear Guilaumin, I am here at the home of a friend.

GUILAUMIN

Oh! This is my nightmare, the National Guard, I left Tours, anything, so as not to join it, ah! A friend, friend, huh! Feminine type, good, you are going to present me then?

DEWORDE

That's why I had you come.

GUILAUMIN

You are really nice: are you sure that you don't hold any rank in the National Guard?

DEWORDE

I hope you will come to my place.

GUILAUMIN

No thanks, cousin, you have too many affairs, I would hamper you; besides, I am coming to Paris to stay here.

DEWORDE

Well! It will be necessary to take a pretty bachelor's lodging, I will make François find you one, and I will send you my draper.

GUILAUMIN

A lodging in my name, ah! Yes, indeed! So they can pity me on muster rolls. No, no, I am lodging with a friend, he will stand guard for the two of us, at Marcel's Rue Tailbout 11.

DEWORDE

(aside)

Marcel, isn't that the name of that gentleman?

GUILAUMIN

Here I am at last. I put in my three days of prison, and I arrive purged of the judgment against me. Now, you promised to present me to a fashionable lady.

DEWORDE

She's dressing.

GUILAUMIN

Ah! That's because I recognized that life is very monotonous thing in the provinces, and I want to make mine gay with follies, or darken it with passions, the heart I am pursing, the woman that I dreamed of is here, and my word, I am going to find her, watch out!

DEWORDE

Still, at Tours, where your merit was known, how the devil did you find—?

GUILAUMIN

Tours is a town which never sweetened the prunes it offered me deceptively.

DEWORDE

Truly?

GUILAUMIN

I am a victim of friendship, I sacrifice myself on this earth, it's true it's for a good comrade, that fellow, a lad who, at college made a duty of what had to be done, and gave the blows I ought to have given, and who not later than two month ago killed an enormous cuirasser who wanted to put me to death, under the pretext I was his rival, a little waitress at the Café d'Étoile, in the corner of the Place du Cours. You know, it's an affair that did me the greatest honor; I was Marcel's witness, then, you understand, as he killed my adversary, the thing made a step in the province, and no one is more rejoiced than I.

DEWORDE

Ah, indeed! How to ever repay Mr. Marcel—you said your friend is Marcel?

GUILAUMIN

I said Marcel.

DEWORDE

Well! How will you ever make a return for such services?

GUILAUMIN

Oh! They are all repaid, in my heart, first of all, since

you see plainly although you are my relative, that I'm lodging with him; and then by good deed for good deed. He's served me in my duels, I have served him in his love affairs.

DEWORDE

Ah! Ah!

GUILAUMIN

That's one of those things that hasn't happened to me, A Parisian, my old friend, a veiled lady, a woman to whom I, I am the confidant, I've never seen her face or heard her voice.

DEWORDE

Truly? And whereabouts was this?

GUILAUMIN

Almost a year ago, but since that time?

DEWORDE

There's been a change?

GUILAUMIN

A debacle, my dear friend, love has melted like thawed ice; so that Marcel has left Tours to follow his inhuman lady, and as for me, I've followed Marcel.

DEWORDE

Oh, why devotion like this?

GUILAUMIN

And of the purest sort, friendship is the feeling of fine souls.

DEWORDE

Silence! Here's Madame d'Illières.

GUILAUMIN

Ah!

DEWORDE

(taking Guilaumin by the hand)

Madame, allow me to present Mr. Guilaumin to you, one of my relatives.

BATHILDA

(aside)

Guilaumin! Marcel's friend?

(aloud)

Sir—

GUILAUMIN

(bowing)

Madame!

(aside)

Heavens, it seems to me I've produced a certain effect.

BATHILDA

(controlling herself)

Sir, you are indeed welcome, presented by Mr. Deworde, and I hope I'll sometime have the pleasure of seeing you. I am giving a little party tonight. Will you do me the honor of being present?

GUILAUMIN

I shall have that honor, Madame.

DEWORDE

It's a costume ball; take a nice costume, dear fellow, and let this ball make a stir, in Tours.

GERMAINE

(emerging from Bathilda's room)

Madame has forgotten her gloves.

GUILAUMIN

Heavens, the old lady!

DEWORDE

What's wrong with you?

GUILAUMIN

That old woman.

DEWORDE

Explain yourself.

GUILAUMIN

Her servant.

DEWORDE

But whose?

GUILAUMIN

Of the unknown lady, the veiled lady, of Marcel's

mistress.

DEWORDE

Marcel! Are you sure of it?

BATHILDA

What are they saying?

GUILAUMIN

You are going to see, I am going to speak to her.

BATHILDA

(aside)

He recognized Germaine!

GUILAUMIN

(to Germaine)

Well, here we are in Paris?

BATHILDA

(low to Germaine)

Deny everything or I am lost.

GERMAINE

Pardon, sir, I don't know you.

GUILAUMIN

Yes, yes, yes, but as for me, I know you; I was a little too bored in our private meetings to forget them.

GERMAINE

Sir, you must be deceived by some resemblance.

GUILAUMIN

(to Deworde)

There you have it, the old girl's afraid this will put her in the wrong with her new mistress.

DEWORDE

(low)

Never mind. Keep going.

BATHILDA

Germaine, save me!

GUILAUMIN

(to Bathilda)

Madame, you mustn't wish her ill for it, this good woman, Huh! She was obeying the orders of her former mistress.

BATHILDA

Germaine has never left me, sir.

GUILAUMIN

(aside)

Great, I've made a stupid mistake.

DEWORDE

Come, Dame, Germaine, reply to the gentleman.

GERMAINE

I can only say what I've said already, the gentleman is unquestionably mistaken, and on reflection, the gentleman will agree.

GUILAUMIN

Indeed, looking at her better, huh! You find these resemblances, Prosper and Vincent, for example. Yes, yes, yes, in looking at her better—and then the other one had mittens and you don't, excuse me, Madame, excuse me. A hundred, a thousand times, I am mistaken, What! It happens all the time. What put me in error was that the other one, the one that resembles you, followed her mistress to Paris, and I was unable to meet her; there are mountains which never meet.

DEWORDE

I don't know anything.

BATHILDA

But all this is foreign to us, my dear Mr. Deworde, and I don't understand the importance you attach to it.

DEWORDE

The name of Mr. Marcel, this resemblance to Germaine.

BATHILDA

Oh! You are offending me!

DEWORDE

I ask your pardon. I am mad.

GUILAUMIN

Well! Here I am in a fine position for my debut! What I'd best do is to withdraw.

(bowing)

Madame.

BATHILDA

Sir, I hope this misunderstanding won't prevent you from returning this evening?

GUILAUMIN

What do you think? To the contrary. Cousin, I thank you for the pleasure you've provided me.

DEWORDE

All the pleasure is mine, I assure you.

(low)

By the way, Mr. Marcel's address.

GUILAUMIN

(low)

I already told you.

DEWORDE

I forgot it.

GUILAUMIN

Rue Tailbout, Number 11.

DEWORDE

Thanks.

GUILAUMIN

(to Bathilda)

Madame.

(He leaves.)

DEWORDE

(to François, who is behind the door)

A letter for Madame.

DEWORDE

You hear, Madame?

BATHILDA

Give it to me.

DEWORDE

I have two words to write, allow me to use this table.

BATHILDA

Do you need to ask me?

(aside)

He's writing I am dying!

GERMAINE

(low)

Courage.

BATHILDA

(to Deworde)

Will you allow me to read this letter?

DEWORDE

Assuredly.

(aside)

Ah! Why, an excellent idea, Bathilda has given me complete freedom to do her invitations. If I were to write to this Marcel?

(he writes)

BATHILDA

(reading)

"If you promised me a rendezvous, you are deceived

in thinking I will content myself with that. I want a positive reply which designates the day and the hour, or, failing that, Madame, I shall have the honor of presenting myself at your home as I did this morning, Marcel." See!

GERMAINE

You must reply.

BATHILDA

What?

GERMAINE

That you will go tomorrow.

BATHILDA

But I am leaving tonight.

GERMAINE

Do you prefer to ruin yourself?

BATHILDA

(sitting)

I'll write.

(she writes)

DEWORDE

(at the other table, reading what he has written)

"Madame, the Baroness d'Illières, has the honor of inviting Mr. Marcel to the ball she's giving tonight, 14 January 1837."

BATHILDA

(reading what she's writing)

"Tomorrow morning at ten o'clock, I will be at your place, but until then, in the name of heaven, make no attempt to see me."

DEWORDE

(to François)

To Mr. Marcel, Rue Tailbout #11.

BATHILDA

(to Germaine)

To Mr. Marcel, Rue Tailbout, #11.

(The two messengers leave by opposite doors.)

DEWORDE

Until tonight, dear Bathilda, until tonight.

(Deworde kisses her hand and leaves.)

CURTAIN

ACT II

The stage represents a small, very elegant boudoir adjoining salons. In two cutaways are two windows, one giving on a courtyard, the other on a garden. In the back, a door, plus two side doors, one giving on the ballrooms, the other on a bedroom.

GUILAUMIN

(alone, looking around him in the Doge's costume)

Now here's the best idea I've had this evening: it's to slip into this little boudoir which appears to me to be reserved for a friend of the house. I'll install myself here.

(lies down on a sofa)

Today I did three things I oughtn't to have done. First, I went to the home of my cousin Deworde, who's a hypocrite and a vulgar man; second, I left poor Marcel alone for the whole day—he's going to call me an egoist; third, I came to this ball, where I bore myself like a Doge, but yet I lost all my money, more than ten francs loaned to me by Deworde, at cards; so that I no longer even have wherewithal to take a cab, which will be necessary, seeing the weather and the costume I'm wearing—it's difficult enough to go on foot.

(he pulls his kerchief from his Ducal cap)

It's an incredible thing. I have a robe. I have two.

(raises a second)

I have three robes and thirty-five ells of material they didn't find a place to put a pocket, while, in my hunting vest, there are nine. Where the devil did Venetians put their money? After all, perhaps they were like me, they didn't have any. A masked ball is not fun: I thought all the women were going to come to intrigue me. Not one came, Still, I have a costume which must attract them. It's Merino, pure Merino. It's true that I only know the mistress of the house, and that she flees me like a leper since my clumsiness of this morning, for, whatever she says about it, it seems to me indeed she has the air of being here. Besides, I'm a bit too annoyed with Dame Germaine for forgetting herself forever or taking someone else to be with her.

O God! Nothing except thinking of my private interview with—with, I am unhinging my jaw tonight with yawning, my word of honor.

But, indeed since I had the wit to discover this boudoir,

why shouldn't I profit by it, all the more as I want to sleep? To think they gave me a narcotic drink to abuse my slumber, what an infusion of poppie heads. Ah, ah, ahhhh, it's very agreeable to go to sleep to the sound of music; as for me, I love music a lot: the thing is to know how to apply it at the true destination. My word, good night.

(dozes off)

DEWORDE

(enters, looking around)

Didn't he receive my letter? Did he suspect something, or amidst all this crowd could he have passed unnoticed? Ah! Oh! Someone's sleeping, my imbecile of a Guilaumin.

GUILAUMIN

(dreaming)

Pardon, pardon, it's diamonds—eight of diamonds, diamonds.

DEWORDE

He's dreaming that he's playing cards, the wretch is sleeping there without guilt, unaware of the venom he released in my heart. Oh! Suspicion, how it infiltrates drop by drop in to the soul to soil it. A thousand times you try to get away from it, cursing its bitter flavor, and always it comes back by a gesture to which you attach a meaning it does not have, through a word to which you give a false interpretation. I have carefully examined Bathilda during the whole ball: she was calm enough, ah! I would give a lot for this Marcel to come.

(a hat hanging above Guilaumin's head falls on his nose.)

GUILAUMIN

(waking up)

What's this?

(picking up the hat)

The fable of the acorn and the pumpkin. If it had also been a schako, I'd have been killed. Oh! Someone! Ah! It's you, cousin? My word, pardon my weariness, idleness, what time is it? Huh? I wasn't able to get at my watch, they didn't put a pocket in my costume.

DEWORDE

They weren't of that period.

GUILAUMIN

Better believe it. You are not paying me a compliment on my costume? It seems to me in the midst of this motley of Pierrots and these odd-shaped mountebanks, it ought to have produced a majestic effect! You see, cousin, we provincials will give lessons in taste to you Parisians.

DEWORDE

Who can doubt it? Tours, especially, my dear Guilaumin. Tours, so rightly called the garden of France, is not only the city of five languages, why it is even the city of fine manners, and without counting you, my dear Guilaumin, who really deserves to be counted, there are still at Tours young folks who could contend with our artistic intelligences and our elegant fashions, aren't there? For example, your friend, Marcel.

GUILAUMIN

(aside)

Great! He goes back to Marcel.

(aloud)

Certainly Marcel is a very distinguished man who would not be out of place anywhere if it were only proven by the choice he made of his friends.

DEWORDE

And his mistresses, because I have a good memory: you said one of our most elegant Parisians had honored him with her kindness, and surely for a woman of such merit and such wit to go bury herself fifty leagues from Paris, she must necessarily find in him someone who had decided her on this exile as a fine compensation for the great sacrifice she was making for him.

GUILAUMIN

(stung)

First of all, my dear cousin, I never said she was elegant, seeing that I'd never met her, nor did I say that she was a woman of wit, since I never spoke to her; as for the word exile that you employ relative to her stay in Touraine, allow me to observe to you that it is most out of place, Tours is situated on the forty-two degrees of latitude and not in Greenland or Kamchatka; communications are easy there, and one gets there by steamboats and stage coaches. You see plainly the ideas you are setting up are contradictory and erroneous.

DEWORDE

I recognize my error about the city of Tours and I make my apologies, but still, my dear cousin, for whatever the lady is, without having seen her, you would have been able to get information about her from her chambermaid. For example, from Germaine.

GUILAUMIN

I didn't say she was called Germaine. It's true I said I was considerably loved in private meetings with her; I insist on establishing the facts in all their precision.

DEWORDE

(aside)

He's determined I shall know nothing, no matter what way I go about it.

BATHILDA

(appearing)

They are together. I was mistaken; he kept his suspicions, this man hasn't left yet?

(aloud)

Well, gentlemen, what's this mean? We have to go looking for you in this boudoir.

DEWORDE

What! In the midst of adding to your preoccupations as mistress of the house, you've deigned to notice our absence, That's too good of you, Madame.

GUILAUMIN

Oh! Truly, Madame. You are confounding me, what! You deigned—

BATHILDA

Certainly, sir. Besides, your costume is remarkable enough to perceive that it is missing in our historic collection.

GUILAUMIN

(aside)

It's always nice to know my costume made an impression; when one spends a 100 francs on a costume, it's annoying not for it to bring you some consideration.

BATHILDA

(low to Deworde)

Send him away, will you? I want to speak to you.

GUILAUMIN

(aside)

I'd really like to leave, I'm not in the habit of going to bed at such hours. Tomorrow I'll be stupid.

BATHILDA

And I, lucky enough, sir, that you were a little amused by this party?

GUILAUMIN

Prodigiously, Madame.

DEWORDE

Yes, I witnessed it myself when I entered.

GUILAUMIN

(pulling Deworde aside, mysteriously)

Hush! No bad jokes—! Say, cousin, rather tell me where I can find a cab?

DEWORDE

Why, would you like me to send François to get one for you?

GUILAUMIN

Ah, you'd be doing me a favor.

BATHILDA

(uneasy)

What are they saying so low?

(aloud)

Gentlemen, is it something that I could—?

GUILAUMIN

Oh! My God! No, Madame, it's simply a question of a cab; for not having the Barge of State, I am forced to content myself with a true cab.

BATHILDA

Oh! That's a plight unworthy of Your Highness. Mr. Deworde, will you take him home?

GUILAUMIN

Heavens! Why, indeed, cousin, you have your carriage; with that, it's only a short trip to Rue Tailbout, Number 11.

BATHILDA

(aside)

He's staying with Marcel!

DEWORDE

It's at your disposition, dear friend; François will have

it brought up.

(The noise of a carriage in the courtyard.)

GUILAUMIN

He! Hold on! Isn't it the one entering the court?

DEWORDE

No, that's Madame's post-chaise.

GUILAUMIN

Madame's leaving?

DEWORDE

At two in the morning: a sick sister in Normandy.

GUILAUMIN

Ah! Really!

(to Deworde)

What are you saying?

DEWORDE

(persisting, deliberately)

Well! But this trip is not a secret, my word! I requested

horses for two o'clock and here they are with great precision.

GUILAUMIN

Ah! For Normandy! Charming country.

DEWORDE

You know it?

GUILAUMIN

No, but I've heard tell it rivals Touraine.

DEWORDE

Well! If you like, my dear Guilaumin, in three or four days from now I am going to make you acquainted with it.

GUILAUMIN

How's that?

BATHILDA

(low to Deworde)

In the name of heaven, will you shut up?

DEWORDE

And why's that, Madame? Guilaumin is my friend, my relative, it's to him that I would make a mystery of your departure and the causes that make you quit Paris. Besides, he's discretion itself and I am sure he wouldn't speak of it even to his best friend, Mr. Marcel.

BATHILDA

(aside)

If he does, I am lost.

DEWORDE

Yes, my dear friend, the thing is still a secret to all the world, but towards you we wouldn't want, we mustn't be so reserved, and if you accompany me to Normandy, it would be as best man at the wedding.

GUILAUMIN

Ah! Madame, I was unaware— What do you mean, if I accompany you, cousin? Why, with the greatest pleasure, if, all the same, Madame permits.

BATHILDA

Certainly, sir, but I ask your pardon for carrying off Mr. Deworde. Would you see, my dear Lucien, if everything is ready while I make a last appearance at this ball? Till we meet in Normandy, sir.

GUILAUMIN

A point of honor, Madame.

DEWORDE

François will come to inform you when the carriage is in front of the hall.

GUILAUMIN

Thanks, I'll be waiting.

(Deworde leaves.)

BATHILDA

Now that he knows everything, he mustn't return home until after I've left.

(She goes into her room without being noticed.)

GUILAUMIN

My, my, my, this sly Deworde hopes getting married like this in secret, and who's marrying—! But he's marrying the one that Marcel loves. Ah, still it can't happen like this; Deworde is my cousin, it's true, but Marcel is my friend, which is better than a cousin, I owe my life to Marcel; all I owe is forty francs to

Deworde for what he loaned me at cards, there's no balance. So, my cousin, so much the worst, my word—but in ten minutes Marcel will know everything, and I have no idea what he'll do; but as for me, I still will have done my duty, if I ought to go on foot.

FRANÇOIS

(entering)

The carriage is here, sir.

GUILAUMIN

Here I am!

BLACK DOMINO

(appearing)

Your highness is leaving?

GUILAUMIN

(astonished)

My Highness! Ah, that's right.

(replying)

Yes, Your Grace, Eh! This isn't bad.

BLACK DOMINO

Now that's a very French response for a Venetian.

GUILAUMIN

It's because I'm traveling a long time in your country, charming cabby, so I contracted all its habits.

BLACK DOMINO

And in your journeys you particularly stopped at ours.

GUILAUMIN

It's the center of civilization; life is comfortable there.

BLACK DOMINO

Witty men.

GUILAUMIN

Charming women.

BLACK DOMINO

Especially those who come from Paris, right?

GUILAUMIN

The Devil! Now what's not likable in your Touraines?

BLACK DOMINO

Still, it wasn't my intention to be unfair to my compatriots.

GUILAUMIN

What! You are from Tours? A native?

BLACK DOMINO

Just like you from Venice, sir.

GUILAUMIN

Now, that's a reply from a mask. You are not from Tours. You don't have the accent.

BLACK DOMINO

What's it matter if I know everybody as if I were there?

GUILAUMIN

Ah, you know everybody there; well, as for me, I bet you don't, I bet you don't know one of these, a young man of twenty-eight to thirty years old, brown hair, black eyes, distinguished bearing who frequents the Café d'Étoile.

BLACK DOMINO

Mr. Guilaumin!

GUILAUMIN

Heavens! My word, you recognized the description.

BLACK DOMINO

And despite this costume.

GUILAUMIN

Ah! Oh!

BLACK DOMINO

Why wouldn't I have recognized him when at Tours they spoke only of him?

GUILAUMIN

As a bad sort, right? The little woman of the Café d'Étoile?

BLACK DOMINO

And as a bad head, his duel with a carouser.

GUILAUMIN

Ah, yes, yes.

(aside)

The Devil! Now, that reminds me of Marcel.

(aloud)

Pardon, but—

BLACK DOMINO

(leaning on Guilaumin's arm)

Alas, a mistress doesn't forget these things, I have really done what I could to drive from my mind the memory of that man, without even being able to do it.

GUILAUMIN

(aside)

Heaven! Now, this is taking a twist. But then, Madame, allow me to tell you that you know ill of this young gentleman. Or do you not know that in Tours and its environs he enjoyed a reputation of cruelty to the despair of women?

BLACK DOMINO

Yes, sir, but how do you expect that at Tours, in a small town—?

GUILAUMIN

Forty-two thousand five hundred souls—

BLACK DOMINO

In actuality, in a province where everyone knows everyone, a woman is going to expose herself; but in Paris it's otherwise.

GUILAUMIN

Well! But we are in Paris.

BLACK DOMINO

So sir, it seems to me that I was even more distant than the rules of good behavior imposed on my sex permitted.

GUILAUMIN

Ah! You won't go as far as I would wish, Madame.

BLACK DOMINO

But what more do you wish? The fatal secret that I've locked in my beast for the last three years, has it not escaped from me?

GUILAUMIN

(aside)

And this poor Marcel, my word, so much the worse.

(aloud)

Ah, Madame, if chance on Providence had made you come to this ball without a cavalier, and if your kindness in its turn caused you to want to grant me this favor of escorting you.

BLACK DOMINO

I am alone, sir.

GUILAUMIN

Then, Madame, can I hope, should I flatter myself, that I have the good fortune?

BLACK DOMINO

Alas! I feel that I am doing something bad, but God will pardon me because he knows how much I am suffering— Well, yes, sir, I accept.

GUILAUMIN

Allow me to offer you my arm.

BLACK DOMINO

Oh, watch yourself carefully, you made such a sensation in this ball that I would be lost if anyone saw us together; in a quarter of an hour, expect me.

GUILAUMIN

Where, Madame? On the stairway?

DEWORDE

No, no, they might still see us. We are at Rue New des Petitro Champs. I dwell in the Faubourg Saint Honoré: wait for me on the Place Vendome.

GUILAUMIN

(cooling off)

At the foot of the column? Ah! Ah! But how will I recognize your carriage?

BLACK DOMINO

I will recognize your costume.

GUILAUMIN

Pardon, Madame, I am going to change it; soon I will have a chestnut overcoat.

BLACK DOMINO

That doesn't matter.

GUILAUMIN

In that case, Madame, in a quarter of an hour.

BLACK DOMINO

At the foot of the column.

GUILAUMIN

At the foot of the column?

BLACK DOMINO

At the foot of the column.

GUILAUMIN

A last observation, Madame, and that I was forgetting because it concerns me.

BLACK DOMINO

Which is?

GUILAUMIN

You see the weather, sixteen degrees below zero and six ounces of snow.

BLACK DOMINO

I won't make you wait.

(The Domino leaves.)

GUILAUMIN

(singing)

Come, sweet lady,

Come, I'm waiting for you.

Hail, gigantic monument

Of valor and arts

Of a chivalrous hue

You alone—

(Deworde enters)

Ah, it's you, cousin Deworde.

DEWORDE

Heavens, you are still here?

GUILAUMIN

Still, the word isn't friendly.

DEWORDE

You told me you intended to leave momentarily.

GUILAUMIN

(humming)

Since then I've changed my opinion.

DEWORDE

And you remained alone here?

GUILAUMIN

No, not exactly, someone had the kindness to keep me company.

DEWORDE

Madame d'Illières?

GUILAUMIN

Ah, indeed, yes.

DEWORDE

Because I've been looking for her everywhere and haven't seen her.

GUILAUMIN

I don't know what's become of her, A single person preoccupies me, and I ask your pardon, dear cousin, if I leave you alone in your turn, but I must follow the eyes of a charming Black Domino, who has placed herself under my safeguard, an Anglican of whom I am the amorous Roland, and furiously amorous! Also, it's necessary that I take a more suitable costume: this one bothers me; consequently, I thank you for your carriage as I have one.

Goodbye, cousin, goodbye.

(He leaves humming.)

DEWORDE

Where can she be? In her room?

(he raps)

Bathilda! Bathilda! Where are you? O no, this begins to worry me. I've searched all the salons for the last ten minutes, and I don't see her anywhere, what's his absence mean? Ah! My God! My God! Why this is a frightful torture, one I've never experienced. Oh, if ever I get hold of this Marcel!

BATHILDA

(entering)

Is it you, Lucien?

DEWORDE

Ah! There you are at last! Where are you coming from?

BATHILDA

Me? Giving orders to Germaine, In ten minutes I am leaving, Deworde, and I cannot express to you how happy I am to leave.

DEWORDE

You are indeed in a hurry to get away from me, Bathilda.

BATHILDA

On the contrary, Lucien, since I am going to wait for you; what do you want? These are forebodings perhaps, but here, I don't see—

DEWORDE

I understand.

BATHILDA

Down there, you see, we will be alone, my friend, no one will come to bother our happiness; it seems to me that only there will I be able to tell you that I love you and how much I love you.

DEWORDE

Oh! Bathilda! Bathilda! If you knew how good you make me feel saying such words to me! Hold on, be frank with me, something has happened to you that you are hiding from me, about this Marcel.

BATHILDA

Again! And in this moment, Lucien, when I am enjoying the happiness of being all yours, when I am not hiding it from you, when I am telling, like a woman, for me to whom such words are forbidden, when I tell you that I love you, what more do you need?

DEWORDE

A complete confidence, Bathilda. A year has passed since the death of Mr. d'Illières and my return. You don't owe me any account of that year, I know that very well, but what do you want? There are shadows through which I seek to see; these shadows, my imagination peoples them with phantoms created by my jealousy. Something which may have taken place during that year will in no way change our plans; that bears no damage to my love; I will not be less your friend, your slave, the one who loves you and will love you before all and more than all; but I will no longer have to struggle with a thousand mad chimeras. Bathilda, in the name of heaven, look, tell me the truth. If some storm threatens our happiness, point it out to me with your own finger, I will help you to protect you from it. Eh! My God! I am a man, I am strong, I can understand anything.

BATHILDA

I have nothing to tell you except that you are mad, Lucien, and obstinate with this skepticism, because what forces me, look? If I loved someone, I would marry that person. I am free, right?

DEWORDE

Oh!

BATHILDA

Rich!

DEWORDE

Too much! My God! I would like to see you poor. I would like to have something to offer you that you don't have.

BATHILDA

There's yet another folly, and then you would be saying that I love you for your fortune, whereas I love you, Deworde, not for that at all, and you cannot have any doubt over it. I love you for yourself, for your honest heart, for your honorable reputation, for your unblemished name. I love you, in the end, because I love you. Have I asked you why you love me? No. I was happy with your love, that's all! Without seeking from where it came, without worrying myself about the past, without fearing the future. Heavens, you are an ingrate!

DEWORDE

How happy you are making me. Yes, forgive me! It's senseless, isn't it, at my age, thirty-five years old, to love this way? It's because you are my first love, because I have so long despaired of possessing you, that I fear to lose you at the moment of possessing you forever. Anyway, our poor hearts are made this way, fearful, even to admit happiness, because they feel that complete happiness is not for them. I ought to fall at your knees thanking God, well! I'm afraid, let me go with you.

BATHILDA

I'd really like that.

DEWORDE

You'd like it?

BATHILDA

No question, and I will be happy that you are not

leaving me.

DEWORDE

Would you really like me to leave with you?

BATHILDA

I was going to ask you to.

DEWORDE

Pardon, Bathilda, pardon! I will accompany you, I won't leave you. Ah! I cannot believe it!

BATHILDA

Well! Then don't hold me back. Let me go change costume, in five minutes, I'll be back.

DEWORDE

Go, go, I am waiting for you, or rather, I'll hurry myself to get ready. Here, soon, right?

BATHILDA

Yes.

(Deworde kisses her hand.)

(She leaves.)

DEWORDE

Yes, I can leave her now. And this Marcel, who didn't even come, I was mad. Let's not lose a minute.

(As they leave by different doors, that at the far back opens and Marcel appears.)

MARCEL

I've got here too late. My head was so completely lost that I didn't return home until midnight, and I found her invitation, which was waiting for me since morning. She must have preferred to see me thus in the midst of company. But that's not my concern, never mind! We'll still profit from the opportunity.

(He puts on his gloves before going into the salon. Guilaumin enters dressed in town clothes looking for his Black Domino.)

GUILAUMIN

The devil take me if I know where my Domino went, not in the salons, not seen to leave, it's fantastic.

MARCEL

(spotting him)

Guilaumin!

GUILAUMIN!

Marcel!

MARCEL

You here!

GUILAUMIN

And you, yourself?

MARCEL

You see, I received an invitation from Madame d'Illières.

GUILAUMIN

And as for me, I was brought here by my cousin, Deworde; I wasn't able to tell you about it since you didn't return all day.

MARCEL

And that's exactly why I came so late; I didn't find her invitation until I returned and then I rushed.

GUILAUMIN

(with comic interest)

Are you rushed?

MARCEL

Certainly.

GUILAUMIN

Poor boy.

MARCEL

Why?

GUILAUMIN

(very sad)

You cause me pain, word of honor.

MARCEL

Why so?

GUILAUMIN

(bursting into laughter)

All the same, it's funny.

MARCEL

What do you mean?

GUILAUMIN

Now there's some nerve!

MARCEL

Will you explain yourself?

GUILAUMIN

Well! The women of Tours are not yet as bold as this.

MARCEL

Will you get to the point, torturer that you are?

GUILAUMIN

Then, it was to say her goodbyes to you.

MARCEL

Who's leaving?

GUILAUMIN

Madame d'Illières: she's there in her room changing costume.

MARCEL

Bathilda! Bathilda's leaving?

GUILAUMIN

Come, come! I wasn't mistaken, it's really she.

MARCEL

She's leaving, and when is she leaving?

GUILAUMIN

In ten minutes.

MARCEL

And going where?

GUILAUMIN

To Normandy, she's going to see her Normandy again.

MARCEL

And what's she going to do in Normandy?

GUILAUMIN

Ah! There we are, what's she going to do in Normandy? I don't know if I ought to tell you.

MARCEL

Speak, I'm on hot coals.

GUILAUMIN

She's going.

MARCEL

She's going?

GUILAUMIN

Well! Listen, my word, so much the worse, she's going to get married!

MARCEL

(seizing him by the throat)

You're lying!

GUILAUMIN

Ah! Indeed, no stupidities; Marcel, you are strangling me.

MARCEL

You lie! You lie!

GUILAUMIN

Eh, no! I am not lying, by Jove, because, because it's my cousin she's marrying.

MARCEL

What's his name?

GUILAUMIN

Deworde.

MARCEL

And who told you all this?

GUILAUMIN

Himself.

MARCEL

He's making fun of you.

GUILAUMIN

But I assure you I know what I'm saying.

MARCEL

Craziness!

GUILAUMIN

And if I give you proof of it?

MARCEL

Impossible!

GUILAUMIN

(leading him to the window)

Look in the courtyard.

MARCEL

Well! A carriage: what's astonishing about that on the night of a ball?

GUILAUMIN

Yes, but a post-chaise, harnessed with post-horses, with a postilion as a coachman.

MARCEL

Oh, my soul, it's true, then; what was the purpose of sending me an invitation?

GUILAUMIN

Are you sure that she sent you an invitation?

MARCEL

Here it is.

GUILAUMIN

It's Deworde's handwriting, the fiancé.

MARCEL

The fiancé! Why this is an infamous joke, and on God! They will pay me dearly for it, ah!

(to Guilaumin, who wants to go.)

Stay.

GUILAUMIN

No, no, all this is going wrong, I know you, you are bull-headed, I don't want to say what animal, and besides, I have a rendezvous, a Domino is waiting for me at the foot of the column.

MARCEL

He will wait.

(he locks the door of the salon.)

GERMAINE

(entering)

Here's your cloak and hat, Madame.

MARCEL

Oh, what an idea! I am making you lose a private meeting, Guilaumin?

GUILAUMIN

Certainly, you are making me lose it.

MARCEL

Well! I owe you an indemnity, Germaine.

GERMAINE

God! Mr. Marcel.

MARCEL

Yes, me, you know me, Germaine; well, your mistress is lost if you don't do, point by point, what I am going to order you.

GERMAINE

Speak, sir, speak!

MARCEL

Put on this hat, this cloak.

(he puts the hat on her head, the cloak on her back)

GERMAINE

What are you doing?

MARCEL

You take this hat and this cloak.

(He gives Guilaumin his cloak and his hat.)

GUILAUMIN

And then what, let's see?

GERMAINE

What's he getting at?

MARCEL

Give your arm to Germaine, get in the carriage, and leave. Here's some money.

GUILAUMIN

Oh! As for that, no, no, no.

(supplicating)

GERMAINE

Mr. Marcel.

MARCEL

You are going to make me do things of which you will repent, I swear to you.

GUILAUMIN

Look, and where are we to go?

MARCEL

Where you please.

GUILAUMIN

That's not a locality?

MARCEL

Guilaumin, I beg you.

GUILAUMIN

If you grab me by my feelings, I'm lost.

GERMAINE

But, sir—

MARCEL

Germaine, I order you.

GUILAUMIN

But—

MARCEL

Remember—

GUILAUMIN

The curses! It's true.

(to Germaine)

Will you accept my arm?

GERMAINE

And where will you take me?

GUILAUMIN

To Tours, in Touraine, and I will say more; I am indeed angry to have left this fine city of Tours.

MARCEL

Are you going to get going?

GUILAUMIN

We are going, we are going, ah! My poor Black Domino.

(They leave.)

MARCEL

Just in time! Now, for the two of us, Madame.

BATHILDA

(emerging from her room)

Just God! Marcel!

MARCEL

Yes, Madame, Marcel!

BATHILDA

(wanting to withdraw to her room)

Ah!

MARCEL

Where are you going? You are deceived, Madame: this is the way your carriage is waiting, and it's through this door through which you husband must come.

BATHILDA

Oh! My God! My God! He knows everything.

MARCEL

Yes, you were going to leave; I am sparing you the shame of it.

(She wants to go to the door of the salon. Marcel locks it.)

MARCEL

Not a step, Madame, you will stay here.

BATHILDA

But he's going to come.

MARCEL

Let him come. That's all I want, my God, let him come.

BATHILDA

Listen, I am asking for mercy. I deceived you, yes, it's true, I intended to leave. Heavens, do what you please. You have my life in your hands.

MARCEL

In that case, you are going to follow me, Madame.

BATHILDA

Follow you? Where to?

MARCEL

Where you promised to come tomorrow.

BATHILDA

Oh, how you terribly abuse my sin, sir, and how, at this hour it ought to be forgiven me, by God who sees what I am suffering; it's because I am only a woman that you are treating me like this. But I have people, I have valets, I am going to call them.

MARCEL

(laughing)

Ha! Ha! Ha! You are mad.

DEWORDE

(outside)

Bathilda.

MARCEL

(rushing towards the door)

Ah! There he is at last.

BATHILDA

(throwing herself before him)

Marcel! Marcel!

(on her knees)

Whatever you wish, whatever you order, I am ready to obey you.

MARCEL

Well! Silence!

DEWORDE

(rapping)

Bathilda, it's me, open up.

BATHILDA

(low)

Where are you taking me?

MARCEL

This window gives on the garden, and the garden has a little gate on the Rue d'Autin.

(He opens the window and sees the snow fall.)

BATHILDA

But will you take pity on a woman?

MARCEL

And you! Did you have pity on me?

BATHILDA

In this weather, oh, but look, I won't go.

MARCEL

(a sting in his voice)

Madame!

DEWORDE

(outside)

You are not alone, Bathilda, I hear a man's voice. Bathilda, answer me, or I'll kick in the door.

BATHILDA

(to Marcel)

You hear him! You hear him!

MARCEL

Come!

BATHILDA

This is really infamous! What are you doing?

MARCEL

Come, I tell you.

BATHILDA

(following him by force)

My God! My God! Have pity on me!

(They leave by the window that Marcel shuts.)

DEWORDE

(breaking the door)

Bathilda! Bathilda!

(he breaks through the door)

Bathilda, where are you?

(running to the bedroom door)

No one! What's this disorder mean? Bathilda, wherever you may be, answer me, if you won't want me to go mad.

(the noise of a carriage leaving can be heard)

What's that noise? Carriage leaving, after having promised me that I would leave with her.

(he rushes to the bell and rings)

François! François! Oh, why this is splitting my head, will someone come? François!

FRANÇOIS

(astonished)

Sir!

DEWORDE

Yes, me. Who gave the order for the post-chaise to leave?

FRANÇOIS

It was Madame—

DEWORDE

What do you mean, Madame?

FRANÇOIS

She just got in the carriage.

DEWORDE

Alone?

FRANÇOIS

With a gentleman!

DEWORDE

You didn't stop them?

FRANÇOIS

I thought it was you.

DEWORDE

It was Marcel, wretch!

FRANÇOIS

The stranger from this morning,

DEWORDE

Yes, but where did they go?

FRANÇOIS

I heard them tell the postilion, Fountainebleau barrier.

DEWORDE

Post-horses with pistols in the saddles, and full gallop.

(They rush out of the boudoir.)

CURTAIN

ACT III

The stage represents a hotel room with a lamp half lowered, side door on the left. Door at the back, chimney to the right in which the fire begins to go out.

Marcel and Bathilda enter covered in snow.

MARCEL

(supporting Bathilda)

Courage, Bathilda, we've arrived.

BATHILDA

Oh! Why didn't I die on the way, in the snow, in a place on the street. I would be less humiliated and wretched than I am to go to your home; this is a shameful and unworthy act you have committed. If I'd been told, I wouldn't have believed it, and yet, I knew you indeed, because I fled from you.

(Marcel lights the lamp.)

MARCEL

Well, in that case, if you knew me, Madame, why did you expose yourself to this violence of which you complain? You knew quite well I wouldn't let myself be deceived with impunity.

BATHILDA

Why? Because I hoped that you would respect enough, if not me, at least yourself, not to use violence, you who are strong, against me, who is weak, because I hoped you would understand that a crime—because it was a crime—doesn't enchain the victim to the perpetrator, because, in the end, I thought repenting to have loved you, to repent it, this virtue of sinners, was permitted me, since it is actually permitted to murderers and assassins.

MARCEL

Ah, you see: in love to repent is infidelity. Because women never repent by themselves; knowing they are weak, they always choose another man to support them in the new path in which they want to enter. While I thought you were repenting in isolation, Madame, I said nothing, did nothing against you, but from the moment I thought I observed that this love was concealing a recent love, I swore that if you were not mine, you would not belong to anyone.

BATHILDA

And do you think this disposes of my fate for a long while?

MARCEL

My God, Madame, it's the rights about which the laws are silent that are recognized by the heart; I had those rights, since you gave them to me!

BATHILDA

By force, sir, as one yields to a brigand who waits for you on the corner of a street, weapons in hand; your weapon is my sin! And with it you intend to kill my esteem. Eh! Yes, I know it very well. What are the rights about which the law is silent? Those who use those rights are infamous.

(She collapses into an armchair.)

MARCEL

Women complain of our strength, but they, they strangely abuse their weakness, they complain that we threaten them, that we force them, oh! They don't threaten us, they don't force us, but with sweet smiles, with soft words they attract us to them. The most terrible become sheep, clipping the claws and teeth of lions, leaving their heads on our shoulders. We drown in their hair, in their sighs breaking our hearts, at the breath of their love, talking endlessly of happiness, of eternity. Then one day, without knowing why, from caprice, and like a feather carried by the wind, they move away, leaving our hearts shredded and beaten, all the more beaten though we are the stronger. Then, if we crawl behind them on our knees, they laugh at us, and if we get up strong and threatening, they call us murderers and assassins. Is it not a mockery, Madame, and the true perpetrators—aren't they the instigators of the crime rather than those who carry it out?

BATHILDA

(shivering)

Ah! My God! My God!

MARCEL

(throwing himself at her feet)

What's wrong with you, Bathilda, what's wrong?

BATHILDA

I am, I'm trembling, how I'm dying of cold! What a fever I've got.

(Marcel wants to take her into his arms, she repulses him.)

BATHILDA

Oh, don't touch me, sir, don't touch me, you said it, I have the right not to belong to you if I am not another's.

MARCEL

(relighting the fire)

At least come close to the fire.

BATHILDA

Oh, while this unworthy journey that you made me take without pity still drags me after you, I've begged God twenty times to send me death, and I hope that he will grant it to me.

MARCEL

Bathilda! Bathilda!

(She turns her head, stops, and seems to faint.)

MARCEL

Oh, her hands, her hands are cold like ice. Bathilda, let me warm them with my lips! Oh! My God! But recall, will you, the times when you yourself came to me without my having to force you to come? Who would have said that a day would come when I would be obliged to tear you from the arms of another and drag you by force? Or a night where you were asking death from God so as not to be forced to follow me? Oh, that one you would have called a false prophet, but blasphemy, senseless blasphemy! And yet hear one at your knees, suppliant, weeping, asking for a word of love, of pity, of forgiveness, and not one word is a lie to emerge from your mute heart and your tightly pressed lips.

BATHILDA

(passing from sigh to sob)

Oh, my God! My God! My God! How miserable I am.

(Marcel moves away from her.)

MARCEL

You are unhappy because you want to be. What has changed in the last year? Your heart, that's all, it's still you, I'm still me, Bathilda, your Marcel. Look at these nearly extinguished ashes. I made a burning fire. Search in your heart: does there remain no spark of love, which through my care, my devotion, my respect reheat into a flame? Bathilda, if you want it, the world is still here, the future belongs to us, no one knows what took place.

BATHILDA

Except he who knows all.

MARCEL

Oh! You are making me think of it; before him it was me, now he is someone else. You talk about what I made you suffer; don't speak then of anything, don't reproach me with anything, you've never been jealous.

BATHILDA

(rising suddenly)

My God!

MARCEL

What?

BATHILDA

I heard noise on the stairs.

MARCEL

It's Guilaumin's voice.

BATHILDA

It's Deworde's!

MARCEL

He must have met him and is bringing him to see me.

BATHILDA

(in anguish)

Hide me somewhere, where you will, just don't let him see me at your place, don't let him know that I came here, I would die of shame.

MARCEL

(opening the door at the back)

This room!

BATHILDA

(rushing in)

Oh!

MARCEL

She loves him! She loves! It wasn't merely a marriage of convenience, it was a marriage of love, ah, but it's the demon who's coming to deliver him to me.

GUILAUMIN

(outside)

Cousin, I cannot go any further, on account of I don't see clearly, only I warn you if you don't put your pistol back in your pocket, I will fire my derringer. I am exasperated in the end.

DEWORDE

(outside)

Are we there yet?

MARCEL

Not yet, gentlemen, but you are going to be there. Over here, gentlemen, this way!

DEWORDE

(rushing in)

Ah!

(he places his pistol on a table)

GUILAUMIN

(at the entrance to the door)

Do you still have need of me?

DEWORDE

No, I've found the one I'm seeking. Go away, Guilaumin.

MARCEL

Yes, leave us alone.

(Guilaumin leaves.)

DEWORDE

You are Mr. Marcel?

MARCEL

And you Mr. Deworde?

DEWORDE

I was looking for you.

MARCEL

I was waiting for you!

DEWORDE

We both love the same woman.

MARCEL

Bathilda.

DEWORDE

Madame d'Illières!

MARCEL

It's the same thing.

DEWORDE

You are mistaken, sir, there is a great difference. I didn't know if she is Bathilda for you, but she is Madame d'Illières for me.

MARCEL

You are very calm and very subtle at the same time, sir.

DEWORDE

That's because I am determined, because I've got you here, because I am sure now that you won't escape me.

MARCEL

And who's thinking of escaping you, sir? On the contrary, be quite certain of one thing: it's that if I hadn't been detained, I would be going ahead of you.

DEWORDE

That's fine! Here we are face to face with each other, a little matter of who has made the whole road. Sir, you love Madame d'Illières?

MARCEL

You are questioning me, I believe.

DEWORDE

I was going to marry her in four days.

MARCEL

In that case, it would be better for me to do the questioning. For my rights are older than yours. You were going to marry her in four days, as for me, I've loved her for the last year.

DEWORDE

I know that, sir.

MARCEL

And who told you that?

DEWORDE

Madame d'Illières.

MARCEL

She told you that I loved her—? In that case, she told you that she loved me also.

DEWORDE

At the moment of contracting such a holy union, Madame d'Illières ought to hide nothing from me, sir; she told me everything. The important thing then is to know not who she loved but who she loves.

MARCEL

What, Bathilda told you that she loved me, that I have letters from her?

DEWORDE

(controlling himself)

She told me that.

MARCEL

But these letters prove that our relationship was most tender.

DEWORDE

I know it.

MARCEL

Most intimate.

DEWORDE

I know even that.

MARCEL

And she told you that during the six months that she was living in Tours, we saw each other every day, that these six months passed like an hour, that during these six months I was the happiest of men, until the day—

DEWORDE

(forcefully)

She told me all that. She's too noble a heart to want to deceive a man who esteemed her enough to want to offer her his name.

MARCEL

She having told you all that, you still persisted in your protestations?

DEWORDE

By accepting me for a husband, she fulfilled all my wishes.

MARCEL

Why, in that case, you were making a marriage of

convenience?

DEWORDE

No, sir, it was a marriage of love.

MARCEL

But you needed her fortune to repair yours.

DEWORDE

I am richer than she.

MARCEL

I no longer understand you.

DEWORDE

(going close to him)

You are going to understand me, I have made a decision.

MARCEL

(ironic)

What's that?

DEWORDE

It's to kill you, sir,

MARCEL

And you still have it?

DEWORDE

More than ever.

MARCEL

Fine! I see we are going to understand each other. What are your weapons?

DEWORDE

Wait, we haven't finished.

MARCEL

What more can you have to say to me, or to hear?

DEWORDE

(exploding)

I still have to tell you that the reputation of Madame d'Illières must remain intact in the eyes of the world, in the eyes of her people, in the eyes of everyone in the end. She disappeared from her hotel tonight. She must return before daybreak or continue on her route. Where is Madame d'Illières?

MARCEL

She's here.

DEWORDE

(hardly containing himself)

Here, in your home?

MARCEL

Here, in my home.

DEWORDE

In that case you carried her off by force; she followed you by constraint.

MARCEL

Freely.

BATHILDA

(emerging)

Oh! That time you lied, sir.

MARCEL & DEWORDE

Bathilda!

BATHILDA

Yes, Bathilda! Bathilda!

(to Marcel)

Who comes to make you blush, you for your cowardice.

(to Deworde)

To thank you, for your devotion.

MARCEL

Let's get it over with, sir. You came to find me, well, here I am!

DEWORDE

A moment yet, sir, I told you we knew who Madame loved, in the past, but we still don't know who she loves today. That's a question that I reserved to make yourself, Madame, and that I am asking.

BATHILDA

What Deworde, after all that has passed, you can still think—?

DEWORDE

Don't I know everything? And are you responsible for the events of this evening, if it is violence which did everything?

MARCEL

Sir!

DEWORDE

Be calm like me, sir; patience, let's wait.

MARCEL

Ah! My God! My God!

DEWORDE

(to Bathilda)

You see, the gentleman's getting impatient. And for my part, I don't want to make him wait too much.

BATHILDA

It's that I cannot believe in so much grander.

DEWORDE

What's speaking to you of grandeur, Madame? But as

for me, I don't know what an honest heart must do. I loved you before the death of the man to whom I owe everything. That man, dying, bequeathed you to me. I ought to have left everything and come to you, to preserve like a treasure this sacred heritage. I delayed. I alone am guilty. But I am not less answerable in the eyes of the world, not only for your happiness but for your reputation, with my love, Madame. You will be, I hope, happy; with my name you will be honored, I swear that to you. Only tell me that on your side, this union, tell me, tell me what you told me yesterday, what you were telling me even tonight, tell me that you love me.

BATHILDA

I will not be less generous than you, Deworde. What you are doing dictates to me what I must do. Perhaps I would have acted otherwise if I hadn't heard all the words of this conversation where each of your responses abased me in my eyes to aggrandize me in the eyes of others. But I owe you so much that I don't want to risk being an ingrate, nor to give you misfortune in exchange for your devotion. Deworde! Deworde! Pardon, but I am suffering more in uttering these words than you will suffer to hear them. Deworde, I honor you like a father, I venerate you like a savior, but, Deworde, Deworde, I don't love you.

DEWORDE

(crushed)

That's the truth you are telling me, Bathilda?

BATHILDA

That's the truth!

DEWORDE

You are telling me this freely, without constraint?

BATHILDA

Freely, without constraint.

DEWORDE

You, you don't love me?

BATHILDA

No.

DEWORDE

Your hand? Goodbye, Madame, I don't wish you ill. I abused myself, the entire fault is mine.

(to Marcel)

As for you, sir, by following here a woman who did not love me, I did a thing I should not have done,.Madame was free in her actions—I wronged you in demanding an account. Her happiness is too dear to me for me not to respect whoever he may be, the one who can give it to her. Receive my excuses, sir, and, and make her happy.

MARCEL

Sir—

BATHILDA

Deworde.

DEWORDE

Goodbye, sir, goodbye, Madame.

(He leaves.)

BATHILDA

(twisting her arm)

Deworde! Deworde! Deworde! Ah!

MARCEL

(on his knees)

But, if you don't love him, in that case you love me?

BATHILDA

You? I scorn you.

MARCEL

Ah! Think that I am still master.

(Guilaumin enters and listens with increasing indignation.)

BATHILDA

You are no longer the master of my life, sir, my happiness is ruined. My reputation is ruined. Oh! I told you: you had made me so wretched that only life remained to me, and you were coward enough not to take it; for blood is paid with blood.

MARCEL

Take care!

BATHILDA

Oh! Now it's I who command,

(to Guilaumin)

Sir, give me your arm and escort me out of this house.

MARCEL

Guilaumin, I forbid you.

BATHILDA

I'm placing myself under your protection, sir. I am calling on your dignity as a man! They dragged me here with violence, they intend to do me violence to prevent me from leaving. Will you stand for it?

GUILAUMIN

Well! No, Madame.

MARCEL

(exploding)

Guilaumin, wretched fool!

GUILAUMIN

Listen, Marcel, I heard everything, and as for me, I have a conscience. I see that you wish to do a thing you have no right to do, an infamous thing! Well! As much my friend as you are, if you take a step towards Madame, I'll blow your brains out, as sure as my name's Guilaumin.

MARCEL

(recoiling)

Oh!

GUILAUMIN

Take my arm, Madame; where must I take you?

BATHILDA

To the Convent of the Visitation.

(Marcel wants to rush to Bathilda, but Guilaumin stops him with the pistols; at last he falls exhausted into an armchair.)

CURTAIN

ABOUT THE AUTHOR

Frank J. Morlock has written and translated many plays since retiring from the legal profession in 1992. His translations have also appeared on Project Gutenberg, the Alexandre Dumas Père web page, Literature in the Age of Napoléon, Infinite Artistries.com, and Munsey's (formerly Blackmask). In 2006 he received an award from the North American Jules Verne Society for his translations of Verne's plays. He lives and works in México.

www.ingramcontent.com/pod-product-compliance
Lightning Source LLC
LaVergne TN
LVHW041626070426
835507LV00008B/466